A HELEN EXLEY GIFTBOOK

EXLEY

NEW YORK • WATFORD, UK

$\mathcal{F}$riendship can only b
measured in memories
laughter, peace and lov

STUART AND LINDA
MACFARLANE

At every stage of my life
friendship has been the
main source of my quite
outrageously enjoyable
existence.

SIR GEOFFREY KEYNES

*By friendship you mean
the greatest love,
the greatest usefulness,
the most open
communication...
the severest truth,
the heartiest counsel,
and the greatest union
of minds of which men and
women are capable.*

JEREMY TAYLOR
(1613-1667),
FROM "A DISCOURSE OF
THE NATURE, MEASURE
AND OFFICES OF
FRIENDSHIP"

*There is no love
so good and so powerful
as the one you find
expressed in friendship.*

SIR LAURENS VAN DER POST
(1906-1996)

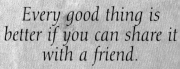

Every good thing is better if you can share it with a friend.

PAM BROWN, B 1928

[Friends] have something you lack, like optimism. They make you feel everything is going to be all right with the world as long as they are around.

BESSIE HEAD

The weary miles
pass swiftly,
taken in a joyous stride.
And all the world
seems brighter,
when friends walk
by our side.

AUTHOR UNKNOWN

*[Friends] are closest to us
who best understand
what life means to us,
who feel for us as we feel
for ourselves, who are
bound to us in triumph and
disaster, who break the spell
of our loneliness.*

HENRY ALONZO MYERS

*... solid friends really are
one of the riches of life.*

JERRY HALL

Ubi amici ibidem sunt opes.
Your wealth is where
your friends are.

LATIN PROVERB

The foundation of true friendship is trust. The building blocks – respect.

STUART AND LINDA MACFARLANE

Friends,
companions, lovers,
are those
who treat us in terms
of our unlimited
worth
to ourselves.

HENRY ALONZO MYERS

*That friendship
only is, indeed, genuine
when two friends,
without speaking
a word to each other,
can, nevertheless,
find happiness
in being together.*

GEORG EBERS
(1837–1898)

Friendships
are our lifelines and
our support system.

BROOKE SHIELDS, B.1965

A friend is there for you
when absolutely
no one else is.

PAM BROWN, B.1928

We cannot tell the precise moment when friendship is formed. As in filling a vessel drop by drop, there is at last a drop which makes it run over, so in a series of kindnesses there is at last one that makes the heart run over.

SAMUEL JOHNSON
(1709-1784)

The moment we [find a friend]... there is no winter, and no night: all tragedies, all ennuis vanish – all duties even....

RALPH WALDO EMERSON
(1803-1882)

The most I can do for my friend is simply to be his friend. I have no wealth to bestow on him. If he knows that I am happy in loving him, he will want no other reward. Is not friendship divine in this?

HENRY DAVID THOREAU
(1817-1862)

A FAITHFUL FRIEND...
WHO WILL REJOICE AT YOUR
PROSPERITY AND GRIEVE
AT YOUR ADVERSITY,
WHO WILL BEAR HALF
OF YOUR BURDEN —
WHO WILL ADD TO YOUR
JOYS, AND DIMINISH
YOUR SORROWS
BY SHARING IN BOTH.

JAMES GIBBONS
(1834-1921)

*She is a friend to my mind.
She gathers me. The pieces
I am, she gathers them and
gives them back to me in all
the right order. It's good when
you got a woman who is
a friend of your mind.*

TONI MORRISON

*I love you for ignoring
the possibilities of the fool
and the weakling in me,
and for laying firm hold
on the possibilities
of the good in me.*

ROY CROFT

A friend accepts you
for who you are,
but expects you to be
all you can be.

RICHARD LOUV

... TO FIND A FRIEND
ONE MUST CLOSE
ONE EYE:
TO KEEP HIM, TWO.

NORMAN DOUGLAS
(1868-1952)

The proper office of a friend
is to side with you when
you are in the wrong.
Nearly anybody will side
with you when you are
in the right.

MARK TWAIN (1835-1910)

*A friend is
someone who can see
through you and
still enjoys the show.*

F. A.

Friends are true twins
in soul; they sympathize in
everything. One is not
happy without the other,
nor can either of them be
miserable alone. They take
their turns in pain as well
as in pleasure; relieving one
another in their most
adverse conditions.

WILLIAM PENN
(1644-1718)

HAPPINESS SEEMS MADE
TO BE SHARED.

JEAN RACINE
(1639-1699)

Shout and everyone
hears what you say.
Whisper and those close
hear what you say.
Be silent and your best
friend hears what you say.

LINDA MACFARLANE

Silences make the real
conversations between
friends. Not the saying
but the never needing to say
is what counts.

AUTHOR UNKNOWN

*If a true friendship
can be found, cherish it like
a fine gem. Polish it, go out
of your way to keep and
protect it. Keep it safe....*

MARY SWANEY

*W*HEN
[FRIENDS]
ARE REAL,
THEY ARE THE
SOLIDEST THING
WE KNOW.

RALPH WALDO EMERSON
(1803-1882)

We have been friends together in sunshine and shade.

CAROLINE NORTON
(1808-1877)

Friendships shape the course of our destiny guiding us through thickets, struggling across burns, and scrambling up hillsides. A tiring journey but the company is good.

STUART AND LINDA MACFARLANE

Friendship is the only cement that will ever hold the world together.

WOODROW WILSON (1856–1924)

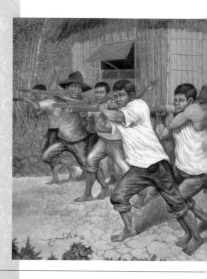

What's the strongest force known to us all? Friendship!

STUART AND LINDA MACFARLANE

*P*art of what friends
experience is something
that people who aren't
friends can't know. It's a code.
It's another language.

JUDD NELSON

Friendship is the hardest thing
in the world to explain.
It's not something you
learn in school.
But if you haven't learned
the meaning of friendship,
you really haven't
learned anything.

MUHAMMAD ALI, B.1942

... with good friends and good food on the board, and good wine in the pitcher, we

*nay well ask, when shall we
live if not now?*

M.F.K. FISHER

As one slowly deteriorates it is very comforting to have friends who are falling apart at the same speed.

PAM BROWN, B.1928

Eggs of an hour, bread of
a day, wine of a year,
a friend of thirty years.

ITALIAN PROVERB

*May friendship, like wine,
improve as time advances,
And may we always have
old wine, old friends,
and young cares.*

AUTHOR UNKNOWN

A real friend is one who walks in when the rest of the world walks out.

WALTER WINCHELL

Friends make it possible to live in a cruel world.

PAM BROWN, B.1928

The necessities of life. Water, food, shelter and a friend.

STUART AND LINDA
MACFARLANE

We want two or three friends, but these we cannot do without, and they serve us in every thought we think.

RALPH WALDO EMERSON
(1803-1882)

Friendship is like the air we breathe. We take it for granted yet need it to survive.

SUSANTA GHOSH

Friendship
is the greatest gift
one person can give
to another.

LISETTE FAVIER

*When friendship deserts
us we are lonely
and helpless as a ship,
left by the high tide
upon the shore.
When friendship returns
to us, it is as though
the tide came back,
gave us buoyancy
and freedom, and opened
to us the wide places
of the world.*

HARRY EMERSON FOSDICK
(1878-1969)

With every true friendship
we build more firmly
the foundations on which
the peace of the whole
world rests.

MAHATMA GANDHI (1869-1948)

There is a destiny that makes
us brothers: None goes his
way alone; all that we send
into the lives of others comes
back into our own.

EDWIN MARKHAM

I said "friendship is the greatest bond in the world", and I had reason for it, for it is all the bands that this world hath....

JEREMY TAYLOR (1613-1667)

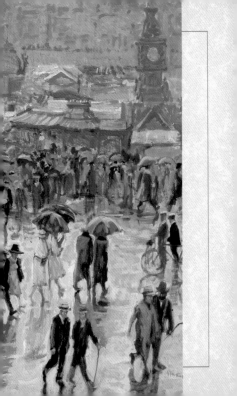

The Beatles knew what they were about when they wrote their song, "I'll get by with a little help from my friends". How else would any of us get by without this stretching out of hands to friends, neighbours, nations?

KAY DICK

*To lose a friend is
the greatest of all losses.*

PUBLIUS SYRUS

*A friend is never forgotten
– even after a lifetime's
absence.*

PAM BROWN, B 1928

*The comfort of having
a friend may be taken away,
but not that of having
had one.*

SENECA

Each human creature
is alone – bound into life
by friendships
– some so small, so slight,
only the lonely prize them
and see their infinite value.

PAM BROWN, B.1928

Friendship needs
no words – it is
solitude delivered
from the anguish
of loneliness.

DAG HAMMARSKJÖLD
(1905-1961)

*It is great to have
friends when one is
young, but indeed
it is still greater
when one is getting old.
When we are young,
friends are,
like everything else,
a matter of course.
In the old days we
know what it means
to have them.*

EDVARD GRIEG
(1843-1907)

*T*IME TAKES
ITS TOLL...
ON EVERYTHING BUT
FRIENDSHIP.

STUART AND LINDA MACFARLANE

*Friends hold tightly
to one another
as time sweeps them
into old age.*

PAM BROWN, B.1928

*Happiness
is the whole world
as friends. It's light all
through your life.*

DANIEL DILLING,
AGE 8

FRIENDS ARE
ALL
THAT MATTER.

GELETT BURGESS

I would not live without
the love of my friends.

JOHN KEATS (1795-1821)

Acknowledgements: The publishers are grateful for permission to reproduce copyright material. Whilst every reasonable effort has been made to trace copyright holders, the publishers would be pleased to hear from any not here acknowledged. TONI MORRISON: Reprinted by permission of International Creative Management, Inc. copyright © 1987 Toni Morrison. HENRY ALONZO MYERS: From *Are Men Equal? An Inquiry into the Meaning of American Democracy.* © 1945 H.A. Myers, published by Cornell University Press. Pam Brown, Susanta Ghosh, Lisette Favier, Stuart and Linda Macfarlane published with permission Helen Exley © 2001.

Picture Credits: Exley Publications would like to thank the following organizations and individuals for permission to reproduce their pictures. Whilst every effort has been made to trace copyright holders, the publishers would be pleased to hear from any not here acknowledged. AISA, Archiv für Kunst (AKG), Bridgeman Art Library (BAL), Bulloz (BUL), Edimedia (EDM), Fine Art Photographic Library (FAP), Superstock (SS), Zefa Picture Library (UK) Ltd. Cover and pages 9 and 36: Edmond Jean de Pury, *Sisterly Affection*, BAL; title page: Frederico Zandomeneghi, *La Lecture*, SS; pages 7 and 72: Peter Hansen, *Petites Filles en Récréation*, EDM; pages 10/11: © 2001 Charles Garabed Atamian, *Beach Scene*, BAL; page 13: August Macke, *Evening Landscape with Three Girls*, AKG; page 14: Walter Firle, *A Good Book*, SS; pages 16/17: © 2001 Gillian Lawson,